SLIPS THAT PASS IN THE NIGHT

The King's English Adrift on the Campus

Compiled by
William W. Betts, Jr.
Professor of English, Emeritus
Indiana University of Pennsylvania

Illustrations by
Stacy Wanchisn Long

ISBN 0-9717475-0-4

Copyright © 2001 by William W. Betts, Jr.

All rights reserved. No part of the material protected by this copyright notice may be reproduced or utilized in any form or by any means, electronic or mechanical, including photocopying, recording, or by any informational storage and retrieval system, without written permission from the copyright owner.

Printed in the United States of America by Laurel Valley Graphics, Latrobe, Pennsylvania 15650.

PREFACE

We are inclined I think to be a little too scornful of the writing of undergraduates. We expect the college freshman to produce a composition that is slipshod and discursive, inaccurate in its observations, incoherent, inept in style or altogether without style, immature, pedantic, just plain dull. But rarely does the student's effort prove to be a total loss. In fact, the contributions made by our college freshmen to English prose are substantial, and many may resist the sweeping scythe of Time quite as effectively as the sonnets of Keats or the ringing rhetoric of Winston Churchill.

Of course not all of these immortal moments are in consequence of a perfected style or a gift for metaphor. Indeed it might be impressively demonstrated that what we desire most to preserve from freshman writing is in consequence of accident. These accidents take many forms: There appear the most shocking misspellings and mistypings, tedious ambiguities and redundancies, confused relationships between modifier and modified, unconscious puns and off-guard confessions, fantastic choices of words, perplexing understatement and bizarre exaggeration, mixed metaphor and bewildering word order, astonishing contradictions and appalling failures in logic.

It is when such accidents tickle the funnybone that the instructor in freshman English comes into his reward. Some instructors, perhaps most, begin to collect these atrocities, and are constantly returning to them to ease whatever pain they may be suffering. Over the years these instructors have been generous with the treasures and have shared them with friends and family and, through publication, with readers everywhere.

This collection got its start at Ohio University in 1954, when one of my teaching colleagues discovered in an essay submitted by a freshman member of a remedial English class this daisy: "Any problems that I had that I didn't want to discuss with my mother, I turned to Alice for advice. She became pregnant at fourteen and dropped out of school." But if it had not been born at that moment the anthology would have come alive with this hilarious student observation, later immortalized in the austere and scholarly Shakespeare Newsletter: "Lear exposed himself to his daughters General and Regional whereupon they cut him off promptly." This inspiration had been preceded some years before by the delight experienced in my reading of the newspaper coverage given the inauguration of Governor John S. Fine of Pennsylvania: "Mr. Fine wore a bow tie—all he ever wears." And by this report, by a biology major, of an astounding natural phenomenon: "The cuckoo does not lay its own eggs." And by the news item relayed to me by the Dean of my college, in which a Detroit physician was quoted as declaring that "nutrition is not a factor in balding, unless the victim is severely malnutritioned."

It was not long before I found myself overwhelmed. Colleagues, as well as friends teaching at other colleges and universities, who knew I was compiling these kinds of howlers, peppered me with fusillades. We were sharing these delights, these fruits of the toil. One instructor wrote to me that in his reading of the student papers he found himself impatient for this kind of satisfaction. He was, he said, "reading with a sharpened appetite. I had become nervously alert." By return mail to him I confessed that I was enjoying the same experience. What a happy moment it is when the student wanders into a perplexing labyrinth of language only to emerge with some astounding vagary, some incredible abomination, some grotesque arrangement of words, which, because of its absurdity, passes at once into the realm of deathless prose. I continued my collecting.

By the time I was ready for the Golden Pond I found that I had been reading college student papers through eighty semesters and thirty-five long, hot summers. Post-mortem calculation produced an astonishing tally: I had read and evaluated 34,172 essays ("themes" we called them) and countless examination papers and research papers. I had by this time assembled, thanks in large measure to my colleagues and teaching friends, some 4000 of these laughers (about 100 a year). These vary of course in their effects upon the laugh-meter. Of these 4000 it might be judged that some 1800 are merely funny. There are 827 which are certainly very funny. And we have 564 which are very, very funny. These 564 are presented here for laughter when you need it.

These boo-boos and boners and senseless atrocities have been organized according to the kind of error which occurs or the kind of subject or situation which has inspired the faux pas. Thus we have those which distort the normal impression of time, and we have those which play havoc with titles of the classics or with characters who appear in them. Sometimes in a single sentence the student will contradict himself; and impossible logic, including the familiar non sequitur, provides still another category. The human anatomy, especially the eyes and the heart, comes in for some rough handling, and the morality prevailing among teenagers is all too rudely described. When the student undertakes analysis of some literary work there is often cause for laughter, and when he soberly attempts an impressive definition the reader needs to secure his safety belt. Sometimes it's merely a case of bad grammar, most often involving a misplaced or obtrusive modifier. Another time the choice of words is delightfully wild, occasionally taking the form of a genuine malapropism or a pun. Striking metaphor is a feature of freshman writing and mixed metaphor constitutes a kind of sub-category. Misspellings of course are often humorous, and even the mistaken computer key makes its contribution. The unconscious confession is always fun, and when the student strives to make a point that is already immensely obvious, well . . . .

Of course arrangement can be a problem, for many of these bloopers qualify for a place in two or three, or four (!) sections at the same time.

The items which follow are almost all the work of college freshmen, though some few come from upperclassmen papers. Many have been inspired by the student critical response to the traditional freshman reading requirements: *Crime and Punishment, Madame Bovary, Moby Dick, Walden,* Shakespeare. In those cases in which the instructor has inscribed in the margin of the student's paper a caustic (or complimentary!) comment—which might always have taken the form of "Really!" or "You don't say!" or "You can't mean it!"—the remark has been respectfully preserved. But in no case has the student's own language been tampered with. The powerful temptation to make the writing even funnier has been steadfastly resisted. Errors in spelling and punctuation have not been corrected, and some selections actually bristle with such mistakes. In two instances, because the humor is pervasive or because so many boners occur, the complete composition has been printed.

A great many campuses are represented here. Among them, besides Ohio University, birthplace of the anthology, are The Pennsylvania State University, the University of Notre Dame, Mary Baldwin College, Dickinson College, Slippery Rock University, West Chester University, and Indiana University of Pennsylvania. Most of the young men and women (perhaps all) who are responsible for these grievances have survived them, and have gone on to fame and fortune. Even the compiler (who has not gone on to fame, or fortune) has his place in the volume, although he is not about to reveal which contribution is his. He will admit only that it is a single complete sentence which was composed in a vacant moment to help out a descriptive essay which was already off to an awkward start and was submitted to a very stern instructor of Freshman English at a small liberal arts college in 1946.

Slips That Pass in the Night is a revised and enlarged edition of the earlier compilation, *A Docketful of Wry*, which was printed in 1970 and again in 1971. For both collections I am most grateful to my many colleagues and friends who with eagle eye and prairie squints have gleaned these jewels from the desert sands, especially the late Dr. Maurice Rider of the Indiana State Teachers College (now Indiana University of Pennsylvania), and Professors William Force and Geraldine Zalazar, whose felicitous classroom instruction for many years proved a productive inspiration to beginning students of writing.

I

ONLY a QUESTION OF TIME

*I consider time as an immense ocean, in which
many noble authors are entirely swallowed up.*
~Joseph Addison

The trailer area in which we were camped was inhabited by many middle-aged couples having children of all ages.

Now about Henry Wadsworth Longfellow, he died at the age of 75 of peritonitis but never gave up interest in life and learning.

The question is not how long the cold spell is going to last but when it is going to end.

After waiting all spring, July 4 finally arrived.

The history-minded historian would say that, due to the practices of the times, Sparks shouldn't be castrated because of the aura of the times, and also because of extenuating circumstances.

After three days of home-cooking, sleeping till noon, and studying when the spirits moved him; he returned to college and continued his interrupted routine.

Clair Conroy died while still being kept alive artificially.

Retirement is busier than before.

The newsman declined to say if cold weather would accompany the cold wave when it struck the city.

He was a tall, bald figure who wore only two suits constantly.

From the age of four months to three years my father was in the Navy and was a complete stranger to me.

Happy were the times when the day endured for what seemed an eternity.

All through my high school career I was a Rainbow Girl. At the present I am inactive.

Least, but not last, Mrs. Elmer Calley spoke to the group.

It is interesting to think that poets from long ago (often dead) can write about . . . what a reader is feeling today.

I spent a day of interminable excitement.

In my childhood I always thought about going to college, but I kept putting it off and putting it off.

His first poem was published at the age of 13.

I reported my findings on a mental record and blissfully left the South knowing that the people of this land are happy to be alive both yesterday and today.

The Department of Highways gave us maintenance personnel this directive: "Inter-state and other heavily travelled highways are to be given priority in your planning; however, secondary and rural routes cannot realistically be ignored until next summer."

Some of my relatives told me how mean my grandmother was after her death.

II

YES aND NO

Do I contradict myself?
Very well then I contradict myself.
(I am large, I contain multitudes.)
         ~ Walt Whitman

Writers who write about the small town very often portray the small American town flourishing with lethargy.

Mom makes the greatest cinnamon rolls in the world, even though she usually forgets to add the cinnamon.

Venice is different in the fact that it is all partly underwater. There is no dry land to be found, not even sidewalks. Despite the fact that the city is submerged, life there is not much different. People still go to the movies, out to eat, to church and out on dates. They have to first call a gondola, which is the name of the boats they use to get from place to place.

Lucetta's victory [*The Mayor of Casterbridge*] did not affect Henchard very much; when he heard she was coming he merely became excited.

There are no authentic recordings of one of these birds [condors] attacking an active man or woman. An unusual event occurred in 1936 when two men were lost in the Andes without food or shelter. They were attacked by a pair of immense condors and one man was killed by being knocked from the cliff by the birds.

My uncle, to me, is an outstanding man. His features are fairly common and his dress is ordinary.

Price of 6 cents stamps to go up.

One cool morning as I was running up the hill I felt a freshness inside me which had lain dormant for several months.

Most of the Middle East countries hate America, especially Nicaragua.   *Contagious, isn't it?*

Nick and Matt both have a big nose, which tends to run in the Italian blood.

I accepted a job in a Y.M.C.A. camp. Naturally I wanted to be liked by the girls in my cabin.

He doesn't walk all over people, but he isn't a domineering person either.

Trite things as kissing or making love to a girl, and hearing what goes on in a pool hall or realizing that your friend is a crook . . . .

The few sounds that can be heard are calm and quiet.

The people must have realized this too, whether or not they were aware of their realization.

I knew it was going to be a lot harder than I thought it was.

The air was warm and humid though at the same time cool and heavy.

A tranquil, unsettled location with nothing around but the smooth, breaking waves and the splendid sound of peace and silence.

The hustle and bustle of the dull, drab everyday life of the city . . . .

The toilet appeared rather normal except for the lack of water present.

He fled when attempting to be apprehended.

He always puts his bat on the ball most of the time.

The sounds were distant, and still.

Sometimes the change is so gradual that it is unnoticed, but appears to be sudden.

I'll be the first to admitte that I'm not the best reader and it's hard for me to keep interested in a novel. But while reading this novel [*Bluebeard*], I caught myself tring to put it down, but I couldn't.

Miss Bradfuss was an excellent teacher. Often when she was translating Latin into English she would make mistakes, and she would laugh and laugh . . . .

[of Elihu in *Job*] His theory of God is one of an all-seeing, all-powerful, and all-forgiving non-entity.

She stood there prostrate with grief.

When Galileo dropped his two unequal balls off the Leaning Tower, he did not physically conduct the experiment.

I placed my parents on a pedestal because they got along so well. Granted they had their little spats and one could hear them all over the neighborhood, but these never lasted more than a couple of hours. Sometimes it was even fun to watch them fight.

. . . marital relations out of wedlock . . . .

Under due process of law the courts established protection for citizens. They have the right to counsel and to a speedy and public trial. Unlawful search and seizures and forced self-incriminating testimony are also given as rights of individuals. *Heil Hitler!*

Dr. Faustus' goals and ambitions are filled with emptiness.

Students these days are more committed and apathetic. 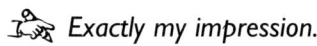 *Exactly my impression.*

The bedraggled fly, trapped in the station wagon, buzzed and buzzed until he fell, exhausted from his effort. I opened the window and the fly rushed to freedom.

One way Winston attempted to perpetuate his thoughts was through a diary. This wasn't illegal in Oceania, but was punishable by death or twenty-five years in a labor camp. *One wonders what the penalty might have been if the diary **had** been illegal.*

I dismissed the recurring thought.

The cottage was set snugly in a treeless forest.

My opinion was somewhat positive to a limited extent.

Although I am not as close to my aunts and my mother as I am to my immediate family . . . .

Language can quite often make a woman seem inferior to man or it can simply make her presence seem invisible.

It's just an ordinary town filled with ordinary people; no other town could ever take its place.

The day was shuddered with advancing night. Whispered silence filled the air.

One night I witnessed a scene which I knew happened every day.

The lifeguards ordered the swimmers to return to the shallow depths.

I live in a marvelous town; the country is really something to behold.

[on Shirley Jackson's tale "The Lottery"] The protagonist in the story is Mrs. Hutchinson. She is calm, and actually one of the more excited and boisterous people at the lottery.

Not all country people are bumpkins. I live on a farm, and I know how to milk a cow, however I live near the main rode, can read, go to college, and occasionally I even hear a news broadcast.

People react to words in different ways. To call a person an animal because he is huge, has a hair-covered body and likes bananas is absurd.

. . . the world renowned chimneysweep . . . .

Mrs. Schultz was a remarkable woman. She was always giving things to people even when she didn't have anything to give.

Poor choice of words. **Remarkable** *isn't the word. Mrs. Schultz is downright gifted!*

[Robert] Frost is unique in that he sees the same things that we see.

Joan was a good-looking girl, friendly to all. But she had one fault; she was unsociable. She would always rush home after school without ever participating in school functions. One couldn't dislike her though, because she was so friendly.

III

WORDS   WORDS   WORDS

*I have made this letter longer than usual
because I lack the time to make it shorter.*
~ Pascal

*In words, like weeds, I'll wrap me o'er,
Like coarsest clothes against the cold.*
~ Alfred Tennyson

*Words are like leaves; and where they most abound,
Much fruit of sense beneath is rarely found.*
~ Alexander Pope

What is tomorrow except the day after today which will be today tomorrow? As each day goes by, do you feel that you have accomplished something to make your day worthwhile so that if it were your last you would be satisfied? Do you go on "living each day as though it were your last," or are you preparing today for a better tomorrow? Can you go on into every tomorrow living for a better one? Live for today and go on into tomorrow satisfied with each day you have lived. You can live today and plan for something for tomorrow, but don't make tomorrow's happening the only thing you strive for. We cannot live only for today as we cannot live only for tomorrow. Live each today and keep your memories and other plans for tomorrow, but don't just live for one great tomorrow which may never come to you. Could you crowd everything you have planned for tomorrow into tomorrow? Today is today, and tomorrow will be another today, so "enjoy yourself, it's later than you think."

Raine was the female heroine in the play.

By the use of voice inflections and believable emotions such as crying, laughing and hushed voices, and background noise make the whole drama seem like a more common story about everyday life.

It was one of those warm summer days so common in summer.

This is truly an important event in my life, which I shall never forget and will always remember.

It is exciting learning of new and innovative ideas of which Mrs. Brewer can answer nearly any question a person would ask.

Emma [of *Madame Bovary*] got a taste of the life of the well-to-do, and she loved it, she craved it, she desired it—she wanted it quite a bit.

Opinions are given all over the world about everything. There are also opinions given about the world and the way it is run. Opinions about other countries, given by other people, are not always true and sometimes the people don't even know what they are talking about.

I feel obliged to concur in your opinion of these opinions.

If there were any man I could turn to, I would go to him and say, "Oh please supply a little meaning to me in my bewilderment." The most dreadful meaning is not so dreadful as meaninglessness, and this is the more terrible the more meaninglessly it smiles.

Being out all night partying and carousing also has a feeling of rebelliousness on the beach without adult supervision and having all the decisions in life up to yourself.

High morale, in this case, proved undesirable as well as fatal.

The rooms were occupied with darkness, allowing the stirs of fear to inflate.

[the extraordinary opening of a freshman's composition]
Beginning with the factor of which most clearly stands outs, the idea watching whatever he or she feels it.

In co-ed housing as well as single sex, all the rooms in each wing are either male or female. The difference in co-ed housing is that each wing on each floor, and alternating on surrounding floors, is a different sex.

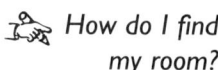 *How do I find my room?*

Not only must the leader be a capable performer but his followers must give him full support along with the other circumstances that go down the ladder of abstraction.

The room had just assimilated the sun which made it appear brighter than usual and seem closer to earth.

We all donned our coats and preceeded out the door leaving an extraordinary, but exciting behind.

. . . if we are going to offer all the things we are offering we may have to eliminate some of the offerings.

Somehow they managed to slip away from the actuality that was encompassing them.

Being an old cabin suggested that we had better go to the cabin and shovel off the snowy roof.

She never told my grandfather, because as any parent in those days, that kind of behavior was quite unacceptable.

I segregate males and females because I feel it interests them differently than it would the general public.

Becoming lost is virtually impossible because the birds whose homes reside in the treetops seem to be leading the way by singing their cheerful melodies that only they seem to understand.

IV

Making the Obvious Clear

An honest tale speeds best being plainly told.
                        ~ William Shakespeare

There are many reasons why death can happen, but the results are the same.

We live in a modern world.

Mr. Delray [the teacher] resented the boy's smart talk, so he hurried down the aisle to where the student was sitting. Taking him by the shoulders, he jerked him out of his seat, asking him if he wanted to be sent through the closed door. He told his class if any of them ever talked back he would send them flying through a closed door, too. Naturally this caused some talk among the students.

Clytemnestra murdered her husband, and that sort of broke up the family.

Our world today is a very complicated one, requiring much thought and study to be well versed on a subject.

The American public is sometimes a disgrace to mankind.

What King Creon does about the disobedience of Antigone and what results from her punishment makes a very tragic tragedy.

Mercury pollution can be extremely fatal.

The forest was heavily populated with huge trees.

I have a friend whose mother drinks booze as if it were water. One day when Fred, my friend, was leaving the house he said, "Mom, I'm going out now." His mother replied in a harsh tone. "I don't give a damn! Get the hell goin'." The love she has for her son did not shine through very brightly that day.

Scenery was everywhere you looked.

Sex plays a very important role in our world today.

After fifteen years of research, David Silvertone is convinced that listening affects an individual and that noise can interrupt this listening ability. *Hooray for research!*

A book must also follow the title.

Many short stories are fiction.

[in recalling teachers and striving for clarity] I never really liked Miss Burgess; in fact I detested her.

As a tiny infant your personality and character will be affected by your environment, your friends, and most of all by your parents.

If it were not for sex people would become extinct.

Richard III was totally horrid for England.

Co-education gives a person a chance to know the opposite sex and other kinds of people.

Single women have found that no matter how much they try to fight it, human nature is only natural.

Luckily I wasn't hurt fatally.

If he didn't like the food, Joe would turn his plate upside down on the table, leaving the food for someone else to clean up. Joe didn't have very good table manners.

There are two sides
to sex education,
a good side
and a bad side.

Ann stood screaming shrilly in the corridor. She was shouting at Linda, telling her she just couldn't stand living with her. another day. She said Linda was downright *impossible*. Ann was really quite outspoken.

Hemingway believed in sex. Frederick Henry [A *Farewell to Arms*] visited the whores in camp; he also believed in sexual relations between men and women. He believed in marriage, too.

Although most people don't give much thought to it unless they are extremely ill or a close friend dies, death is inevitable to us all. This is especially true of people my age.

You can learn a lot about war especially if you have participated in it voluntarily or otherwise.

Between the years 1861 and 1865 the city of Richmond was under the influence of the Civil War.

No family is complete without a mother.

From my point of view, all human beings are conceived and from then on have a life ahead of them.

When I read "Stopping by Woods on a Snowy Evening" I often think of myself stopping by woods on a snowy evening.

I consider my mother irreplaceable.

Another thing that really caught my eye that was the ads for cars in the 1969 issue [of the *New York Times*], because there were absolutely zero ads selling cars in the 1869 edition, possibly because the car was not invented.

My hometown will probably never be remembered as a link in the history of my country.   *No, it probably won't.*

[the student recalls a former teacher] It was not unusual to find him suspended from a hook in the coat room or locked helplessly in the clothes closet. One day a boy even hung him out a window by his heels. Sometimes it was a bit difficult to respect Mr. Mclaughlin's authority as a teacher.

The town of Mill Run was little known until about 1958 when it was discoverd that it would soon become the center of a vast reservoir which would supply the entire Pittsburgh area with fresh water. Of course this was rather exciting news for the people of Mill Run. For one thing they were afraid they would lose many of their friends.

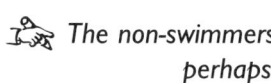 *The non-swimmers, perhaps?*

The buildings in my town are conventional in structure, but the people are all different.

My mother is certainly not perfect. Once when baking she added 1/4 cup of sugar when she thought the recipes said 1/2 cup. It really said 1/3 cup.

V

The Ethics of it

*Indigestion is charged by God with
enforcing morality on the stomach.*
~ Victor Hugo

My girl is a real good girl. She does not take part in the many activities which amuse the not so good girls. When at parties, she always thinks of the most wonderful games to play. Pin the tail on the donkey and apple bobbing are fine examples of her taste for games. Her personality is also very pleasing. She never talks about anyone when he is within hearing distance. Honesty is one of her strongest virtues. She never steals from her close friends. If all the girls in the world were as nice as my girl, this would be a wonderful place in which to live.

Ralph wasn't stuck up at all; in fact he was familiar with all us girls.

There are lots of reasons for teen-age drinking. Recently there was a case when the cause was nothing more than the death of a parent.

One thing that had been preached into me, was never to go through anyone elses things, especially, while I was babysitting.

Sue's father seemed like one of the gang. He fooled around with us girls a great deal. He was really quite different from most fathers.

Danielle didn't approve of my new tactics so she had some of her friends tear down the majority of all my posters, she even spreaded bad roomers about me.

I decided it was better for a mother not to act like a girl friend and likewise for a father.

I was fortunate, or would you call it misfortunate, to pass several tests without preparing for them.

We celebrated the victory game over banana splits.

Especially do I agree with [Bertrand] Russel's views on adultery. Adultery, if committed when a man has been away from his wife for long periods of time and if there is no intimate relation with the woman in the act, does not seem wrong to me. *It does not seem wrong to me either.*

I don't think their is anything as holy and sacred as the love between a mother and child. To the mother the child is a part of her and is a representation of the love that she and her husband have shared—a part of each of them rolled up into one piece.

[Benjamin] Franklin was not truly a moral man, but this, also, was influenced by the age where women were not to be considered but after he had jilted the girl he did come back and marry her.

[student's end-of-course evaluation] My writing, in my opinion stayed the same. I think that if I had better topics [chosen by the student] and knew just exactly what was expected of me, I could have done much, much better. Also I am more confused than ever because my known definition of a verb is completely different than what you say they are.

Many people do not understand sex fully and therefore tend to avoid it in conversation.

The chief of police in my town is a good friend of mine. Sometimes when he sees me speeding down the highway, he will shake his finger at me and laughingly remind me to slow down before I kill somebody.

I felt guilty for being dissatisfied with my mother and not loving her enough, so in order to ease my conscience I gave up comparing her to other mothers and instead wished she were more like my aunt.

Another moral is abortion which is now becoming accepted. [First moral noted in student's paper was untidy dorm rooms.]

My grandmother would remember any offense she thought was committed against her. For instance, she never forgave mother for marrying father.

Two other goals I achieved and which I was proud of, are my girl friend and my car.

The only womanly attribute allowed women in Utopias is to bear normal, healthy children; and she does this for the state. I am not saying that a woman's place is in the home only that her place *is* [italics not mine] under the man.

[life in East Butler, Pennsylvania] Jack's fiancee came into the restaurant and bought a milkshake. While drinking the shake she noticed a note beside her that was put there by Jack; it read: "I just spit in your milkshake." Upon reading this note, Jack's fiancee was so upset she got off the stool and vomited on the clean floor.

They also talk about me behind my back, which is something I would never do.    *Good for you.*

I suppose my father did about as much as any father does at Thanksgiving and Christmas—nothing.

I want a "A" in my English class to show that I have achieved understanding, intelligence & developmental growth.

I now realize that two guys can be good friends and still go steady.

The average parent realizes that incest exists, but they do not want such things to happen on a school stage.

May I say as a friend—that I enjoyed the course, although I didn't attend all of the classes. I read all of the required books, plus Fanny & Zoe which I think helped broden my education in such things as vocabulary, english, and understanding—and may I add I learned some new swear words which may be useful when I receive my grades.
        Sincerely,

If there's one thing that most people question in most people, it's moodiness, especially in your wife.

My knee is at the top of the list for my greatest misfortune along with the death of two of my best friends.

A man is reluctant to laugh at himself if he has tendencies toward adultery.

Even though I set and think,
My hopes for answers sink and sink.
So with the hour drawing neigh
I'll take my "F"
And say good-by.

The grade is "F"; be not distraught. At least you didn't get a nought.

Any problems that I had that I didn't want to discuss with my mother, I turned to Alice for advice. She became pregnant at fourteen and dropped out of school.

The fights at the Knotty Pine Inn are usually over something silly—like a girl.

A virgin is trying to run away from nature. She is being chased by Harvey, a person who wants to get her. She runs into the forest where she felt she would be safe. However, Harvey was near and heard everything that she said aloud to herself. She was reassuring herself of her unusual manner of behavior.

The trial concerned John Scopes teaching evolution in the classroom instead of the Bible's version where man and ape were not the same.

Love is a part of nature and it helps to protect its young. Nature provides a concealment or hiding place for the young virgins. This was one of Nature's first duties.

    Dear Professor—
    I just received the B grade for the course. I want you to know I earned an A in that course and that is what I expected. I am not satisfied with your grade at all and I want you to know it. *I do not accept your grade.*
                                    Sincerely,

VI

True Confession

*It is a maxim with me that no man was ever
written out of reputation but by himself.*
~ Richard Bentley

Confession of our faults is the next thing to innocency.
~ Publilius Syrus

Every man has his faults, and honesty is his.
~ William Shakespeare
Timon of Athens, Act II, Scene 2, line 170

If you are 12 years old and if you want to make a trip to Canada for the purpose of fishing; who may I ask, is a better comrade than your own father. He has a car, fishing tackle, camping gear . . . .

I would like to be excused from your class on Friday because I have to be a pall-bearer at my brother's wedding.

A car was creeping behind me. It seemed to be coming at a terrific speed.

To make this trip [through the Grand Canyon] costs ten dollars. I did not have time to make it.

I thought I was a half descent writer up until I came into your class.

An occasional dog noticed my uncertain gait and winding path up the middle of the road, but must have remembered me . . . .

VII

Eyes, Ears, Nose and Throat

Who stabs at this my heart, stabs at a kingdom;
These veins are rivers, and these arteries
Are very roads, this body is your country.
~ Stephen Phillips

He wore dark glasses and was seldom seen without a suit on.

[excuse notice to instructor] I did not feel good when I got up. After breakfast I felt worst, and on my way to class I lost everything. Upset stomach is my reason for absence.

Next, my eyes fell on the beds.   🐿 **Was this before contacts?**

There was a feebly growing down on his chin.

I got out of the truck and checked to see if my friend was all right. Finding out that he was all right, we started to walk up the road to see what was going on. My legs felt like rubberbands and I think my stomach was lying on the floor of the truck.

[on describing the setting up for a carnival] As the men piled up the parts for the fairest wheel, my ears would ring as they banged together.

My eyes glided across the field and came to rest on the old, brown barn.

My feet slowly walked up the winding stone steps.

The hospital spokesman said she had suffered at least two broken legs.

Reclining on a cozy sofa, situated before a roaring fire, very relaxingly sipping on a mug of steaming hot cocoa, my eyes drifted out of the frosty windows of the ski lodge.

[of the student's instructor, Professor William Force] He speaks slowly but forcefully, occasionally waving his eyebrows for emphasis.

My exterior appearance is a male with red hair standing approximately six feet tall and weighing 170 pounds.

Her eyes were pools of soft blue which had the capacity to enlarge and cut you to pieces. At other times they would dance with poise.

A glow of contentment spread over his stocky figure.

He longed for the compassionate touch of his wife's voice.

As you step through the door the fireplace strikes you in the eye. *What a pity!*

My heart broke into small pieces and fell to the bottom of my stomach.

Tom found it difficult to turn his back on what was in his heart.

[in describing Mr. Orlidge, who had a glass eye] He seemed to walk sideways all the time with his good eye faced in the direction he was going.

[central image in an essay descriptive of a man's face] Moving down his face is a nose.

We talked mostly to him but he answered us without a word spoken through his eyes.

She stepped back to get a look at herself from the rear.

A sigh was felt as two protruding eyeballs travelled from the pile of luggage to the elevator.

Her eyes skimmed across the room

[from a final examination essay on Loren Eiseley's *The Immense Journey*] The skull expanded to allow a greater mass to develop, a mass of gray matter that was to become the seat of the future generation of man.

He would walk to the front of the room and then wait to see if our eyes were following him.

[David] Garrick's facial features were very good for acting. Under his ruffled brow one could see a happy intellect.

As I heard the screen door creak shut behind me, my eyes fell upon the street in front of their house.

The operator of the sports car then crashed into Mrs. Wilomat's rear end, which was sticking out on the road.

Her eyes follow him from underneath a soiled baseball cap.

His short crew cut looked rather foolish on his monkey-shaped face.

As we settled into our seats we could feel his eyes traversing the room.

As he entered the room, his thoughts were plainly seen in detail.

I felt her eyes fastened on me as I left the room.

VIII

Pure Poetry

*The greatest thing in style is to have
a command of metaphor.*
~ Aristotle

Then there is the case of the unexpecting husband who learns that his wife is going to have a baby. His wife's words make him feel as if he had been knocked over by a steel beam. He quickly reclines in the nearest chair and wonders how such a thing could be true.

As the red sky settles into the seabreezed horizon, an aspiration of spending the rest of the summer eves right here lures within the heart.

The grinding teeth of society cut into his rationale.

A father is not just one of the many elements mentioned in the preceeding paragraphs, but all these elements are put into a huge melting pot, heated and stirred, and the final result is a father.

It ended up that everyone got a zero on the homework and a sore butt to boot.

Grandmother always had that neat appearance; she looked as though she had just stepped out of a shower.

As the moonlight shines on each wave floating to shore, and the gentle breeze blowing about, one can feel the gracefulness, comfort and glamor of the beach during darkness.

When the Servian officer came through the window, Raine did not become worried. He seemed to her to be a fairy princess . . . .

The sea itself looks like a piece of blueish green silk accented with an occasional ripple or two. It extends so far. Seeing when the sea ends seems impossible. The wonder of if it really does and crosses the mind.

Tension crackles through the air.

Her personality was a unique triangle—one of beauty, brains, and talent.

A warm summer night, once the gleam in a woman's eye, has but vanished escorting the brisk weather of a cold October day.

King Charles walked and talked; a half hour after, his head was cut off.

As the street lights of the sky beamed down upon the water, looked like a large silk sheet.

The darkness of the night could be seen through the flashes of spark appearing as the commotion continued.

[image inspired by the student's reading of Ken Sobel's *Babe Ruth and the American Dream*] It remains a squalid, half tar-paper shack, half crumbling brick wreck of a building, with windows of chicken wire and roaches two inches long.

Even as the soon-to-be-born child emerges from the womb, the dark all-encompassing cloud of competition in society engulfs his small mind and body, striving to obtain control of even this, the tiniest and most untarnished of souls.

I felt like a fish in a sandbox.

IX

Mixed Metaphor

Confusion now hath made his masterpiece.
      ~ William Shakespeare

The comment "It's a long tomorrow" truly hits the bulls-eye on the nose.

But the rut the housewife will eventually fall [into] is a rising problem in America.

I became a black sheep in the crowd, sticking out like a sore thumb.

The captain was eaten up by the seeds of doubt.

If we could look into the eyes of the people behind the Iron Curtain, we could see a hidden warmth in their hearts.

[discovered on a note which was intercepted on its way from one student to another] The old buzzard is watching me like a hawk.

X

LiTeRaRy CRiTiCiSM

Break your worthless pens, Thalia,
and tear up your books.
~ Martial

[in explaining the significance of Andrew Marvel's lines "The grave's a fine and private place, / But none, I think, do there embrace."] This quotation means that the grave is quiet and nice, but it is lonely. Nobody will ever enter into your grave.

[concerning the first meeting between Jim Burden and Antonia (in Willa Cather's *My Antonia*)] They went to the haymow to get to know each other better.

This is what Hamlet does—he does not act.

[opening comment of a student's analysis of Emily Dickinson's "After Great Pain a Formal Feeling Comes"] I think that this poem was written during a period of war because of the line "This is the hour of lead." Lead is a common nickname for bullets.

[on poet Edmund Waller's lyric "On a Girdle"] The speaker is willing to trade everything else in the world for that which is contained in his girlfriend's girdle.

"The course of true love never did run smooth."—spoken by Lysander to Hermia. [*A Midsummer Night's Dream*] Foreshadows the action of the lovers and how they are finally maneuvered into the correct positions.

[inspired by George Orwell's "A Hanging"] However, he goes home and shares a drink with the dead man 100 yards away.

If Hamlet could have triumphed over his excessive disorders, we may have had another Shakespearean play to add to the rostrum, *Hamlet, King of the Danes*.

[uncovered in a student's analysis of John Donne's "Batter My Heart" (Notre Dame, June, 1963)] This English sonnet is a petrarchan or Italian pattern. The reason I think it is an English sonnet is because labor in line six is spelled the British way, "Labour." It is an iambic pentameter sonnet. The feet of the sonnet have duple meters, and there are five feet to each line. The sonnet is written by a man, as the rhyming words are one syllable each, which is a man's style.

[on Thornton Wilder's *Our Town*] He has put faceless people on an empty stage and has created timeless lines from their mouths.

Eventually Emma's Achilles heel [*Madame Bovary*] is brushed by the silken cuff of a dandy, and down she plunges.

Treasure Island is a fiction novel which takes the reader back through the ages until the period of John Silver and England is reached.

[on Henrik Ibsen] After his death in 1906 he became quite popular, as did his works.

[on poet Edwin Arlington Robinson's Eben Flood] He liked to drink according to the poem. He had a party with himself and he was very gentle with his jug. He was a lonely man.

[Shakespeare's Iago and Emilia] Since he did not receive the position he wanted he was very insecure. In other words, "he had trouble at home and at the office."

George Orwell is faced with this pressure when a Dravidian collie is trampled by the elephant and the alarmed public anticipate the death of the beast.

Richard Cory was a person to whom everyone looked up to. He shot himself because money isn't everything.

Thoreau said that clothing was irrelevant, that all a man needed were the bare essentials.

[Iago again] Before he stabs her in the end . . . .

[on D. H. Lawrence's poem "Piano"] I think I detect the unsavory shadow of homosexuality in "manhood cast down" or at least something less than normal, and I imagine there may be Freudian overtones in "great black piano" which I do not even want to know about since I have always loved the piano.

The Hairy Ape describes the individual in modern society as a man who resembles a gorilla and should be locked up.

Such books as *1984* and *Brave New World* aren't really harmful if they aren't taken too seriously.

William Shakespeare in his play *Richard II* used such terms as "precious stone set in the silver sea," "blessed plot," and "this fortress built by Nature for herself" to describe England, a middle-sized island of frogs and rain, a land studded with smoke stacked cities and rocky highlands.

I appreciate what [poet Ted] Hughes has done in "View of a Pig." He has crammed everything he possibly could in to it—and more.   *Hallelujah!*

I was reading *Walden* last night; it's about this . . . pond.

I think we could say that Canadida suffered slightly in self absorption in that she needed reassurance as being an attractive woman. But I also feel that this was largely due to her entering her middle-ages.

George Orwell was predominantly a novelist. He was born and raised in India, in 1903.

When Adolph Hitler published his book, *Mein Kampf*, the world read it with an open mouth. When the book was closed, the world's mouth was too.

[on Henrik Ibsen's Hedda Gabler] Hedda is an unkind woman who wants to be in charge of someone's dynasty.

A play dealing with incest could be presented to an adult audience where the acts of incest and adultery exist.

There are husband-wife killings today, but few are based on reason, like the one in *Othello*.

I have started many books, but have never finished them because of the people in them.

[in discussing *Les Folies Bergere*] It was the greatest performance of everything that I ever witnessed.

[on Andrew Marvell's lyric "To His Coy Mistress"] This passage is very anti-courtly love oriented. He [the poet] is very anti-courtly and makes references to vegetables.

In *A Farewell to Arms* sleeping together is a common thing to do.

Even after Thoreau had brought his crude type of civilization to the pond, all of the harmonious instincts of nature remained.

Bret Harte's humor is a type of quiet humor, I would say, that comes to light in a pitiful way.

The husband of Anne Hathaway was Mr. Hathaway.

Mr. Mitty had the type of wife which didn't help his condition.

In the essay "Decency and the American Novel" he [William Dean Howells] tries to stress that sex is not an everyday occurrence and that it can be eliminated.

Troilus and *Criseyde* are novels by Chaucer. The later being the more important.

[Thoreau on shelter] As long as he was still able to squat he did not see the need for building laboratory facilities in the house or outside.

[on the poem "And Love Hung Still," by Louis MacNeice] The man is speaking to the woman in bed with him, which I assume is his wife, or some other one-night lover.

[in discussing *The Glass Menagerie*] Amanda wanted to feed her children nourishment on which they could grow, but the evils of life caused her milk to sour. Laura, too fragile a creature to digest sour milk, blowed out her candles and mentally died.

XI

The Classics

In glorious titles he excels.
~ William Shakespeare

"The Soliloquy of the Spanish Oyster"

"Two Tramps in a Mud Puddle"

The central figure of *The Scarlet Letter* is Sahara Preen.

King Leer

Milton wrote "El Ponderoso."

[Oedipus Rex] Edipace Wrath

XII

LET'S DEFINE OUR TERMS

I hate definitions.
~ Benjamin Disraeli

A psychologist is a man who pulls habits out of rats.

A fiction book is just a lot of words shuffled around to make a story.

Heaven is windy paths paved with gold.

A courtesan is a lucid woman.

Aristotle: a Greek philosopher who said "I think therefore I am" and later drank poison.

[a definition of theme] What a story is all about. The jist of the story. The meaning. The theme of Little Orphan Annie is the struggle to survive by a girl with no eyes in a world of people with eyes.

Poetry is a different way of telling the world about the life around us. It is said in quite a different manner and this manner consists of verses, stanzas, and many other forms of poetry. Sometimes we can understand it and sometimes we can't. It is a form of literature, whereas there is a definite rhythm of reading and in many cases a definite form of composition.

[on child abuse by parents] Sexual abuse is the incest between obedience and integrity.

[on Maurya, the heroine of John Millington Synge's *Riders to the Sea*] This woman straddles Aristotle's definition of a tragic hero.

Metonymy: use of the specific to suggest the general. For example: the penis, mightier than the sword.

Most people think of a square as having four equal sides shaped like a rectangle.

A platitude is a level stretch of land lying between two mountains.

Euthanasia is a situation where the patient ends up dead sooner than he or she otherwise would.

[definition of *picaresque*] Making something obscure big to give some style to the writing.

Pestilence—person with no enthusiasm about anything.

The *skene* is the portion of the theater where the actors exhibited their parts.

Catharsis occurs when the spectator gets everything off his chest and leaves the theater thoroughly cleansed.

Restoration tragedy characterized by excessive spectacle, bombastic dialogue, violent conflicts and exotic settings was known as Elizabethan tragedy.

[from a discussion of levels of abstraction in a class on semantics] Instead of a large brown and white animal with utters that goes "moo," high level abstraction would simply call it a cow.

[*Our Town* again] Death is a venture. Just as we venture into mischief or venture to another country, we venture into death.

[courtesy of Mary Baldwin College—student response to the request for a short definition of a typical family] A typical family consists of a father and a mother and the children born out of their wedlock.

Stonehenge: a pile of old rocks in the southwestern part of England.

XIII

ORTHOGRAPHY aND IBM

As our alphabet now stands, the bad spelling,
or what is called so, is generally the best,
as conforming to the sound of the letters and of the words.
~ Benjamin Franklin

To punish herself for this she pubicly admitted to her sins each week in church, and then distributed the profits to the people.

Ancient people made sacrifeces to their gods.

Actually, A & P stands for the Great Atlantic and Pacific Teat Company.

Please mail me my bount copy of my thesis.

The young people of the church agreed to sit down for a pet-together with some of their senior citizens.

. . . title waves . . . .

It is good that morals do not have the power of God.

Baptist by birth, even though he confesses he would probably be Baptist even if his parents weren't, Donnie still takes time to prey.

. . . rumour mongrels . . . .

She intently poured herself over her work.

~ 57 ~

She was noted for her ability to work hormoneously with others.

This is just one example of the loss of respect for women. I don't feel we should be put on a pedal stool.

Think for a moment about the case of Mr. X, who works in the local furniture facture.

Uncle Melik [William Saroyan's "The Pomegranate Trees"] tried to make a flowering garden out of the dessert but failed.

. . . unless we are unable to practice because of the in-climate weather.

. . . lopped sided shopping cart . . . .

[comment on the opening lines of Milton's *Paradise Lost*]
Milton is asking for the blessing to amuse and is telling how death came into the world by disobedience.

Cortex was a mistake, because he was a Spaniard that conquered Mexico.

Needles to say . . . .

Russian writers were much concerned with the rising of the surf.

The nuns observe strict enclosure, according to the scared cannons and the special regulations of their order.

A characteristic of the folk ballad is that it was written by the pheasants.

Americans would be happier, more content with their lives, if they gave more attention to hymen relations.

People with their extra time have different interests so they have different ideas on how to spend their leisure time. Many people watch T.V., some like to read, but most of all there are those who are interested in spats.

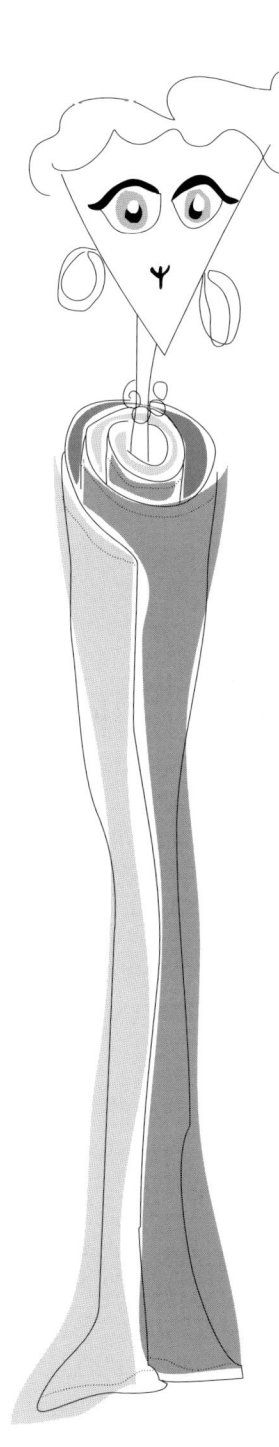

There stood Gloria rapt in a Turkish towel.

So when you become open-minded you must remember to have humility and think of others before sprouting off.

Oswald, in Ibsen's *Ghosts*, is suffering from congenial syphilis.

With his rough, calloused hands my father grasped the scared bible.

As we left the car, the wind swept us up the walk and into a world pool of leaves near the door.

To this day I am impatient with people who call Negroes off-colored names.

My parents had brought me upright.

The U. S. as a nation, has a fear of Russia and its *Sputnuts*.

. . . a chance to witness an enbombing . . . .

She was determined not to travel with him, for his reputation was as a wreckless driver.

I was so cold I was ridged.

His possessions he could probably get through a knot whole, but he was happy.

The Iroquois accomplished this enormous feet.

The physicians could not heel them.

They tried to wart off the disease.

[on Hemingway's story "The Killers"] Nick thought it [death] was offal.

In 1937 the American Medical Association endorsed birth control pubicly.

Dan had stopped breathing and was now in a comma.

To get milk from a cow we pull and squeeze the utter.

Billy Budd was cast in many rolls.

People often take for granite things which they should think out slowly and carefully.

Since he was very ill he was given his last rights.

Misfortunes can be conscrewed by some characters just as grief.

Time pasted quickly . . . .

When an accident is described to me I can picture it and I always shutter.

A new error of transportation began when the Wright Brothers took off in their flying machine.

The main point is that there was no love lossed between us. 🐛 *Thank heavens for that!*

It was to great for him to bare.

Atom was the first man writ about in the Bible.

I feel a lot of problems of today's society is caused because of our laxidaxic communication skills. 🐛 *I suspected many causes but never laxidaxicity!*

Musical entertainment was provided by Ellie Derk, while Bill Jackson played the strumpet.

Edward is a character in a middle age ballad.

Everyone is all raped up in their bulky coats.

There occur in *Moby Dick* a quotation from the *Conversations* [*of Eckermann*] and a reference to Eckermanan's description of grazing on the corpse of his beloved friend.

Canevin [High School] made me and my fellow teammates feel like we were taking place in Custard's Last Stand and there was nothing we could do to stop it.

But the story of farming on the plains is a sad one, with most of the farmers ending up with a dust bowel as a farm.

A polka-a-dotted bow tie completes this outfit.

Often movie stars present themselves in a fascinating manor.

If you want to destroy the old factory nerves . . . .

Because I lived in an icelated corner of the world . . . .

XIV

WHAT LOGIC

It is well to test everything.
~ Sherlock Holmes

We don't believe in executing the insane because they won't learn a lesson from it.

Katherine Anne Porter is trying to put across the idea that death can be a hindrance to life.

Starlit beach memories reflect perfection at its very best.

Eisenhower has consistently tried to raise the standard of education for every American regardless of race, creed, or nationality.

I came from a family of only one child.

I always thought that a man became a priest if he couldn't do anything else or if he didn't like girls.

I have learned that the first step in choosing a campsite is determining where you want to camp.

His not being able to swim was the effect of his drowning.

She was happy as always but not in the same way for she had married the month before.

The novels of William Dean Howells were without reference to sex; therefore they were popular with young girls.

The value of lighthouses cannot be measured by mariners who have been lost at sea.

The unexpected is something I can't foresee.

When I woke up, my roomate was asleep which meant that his freinds had been there and I wondered to myself when were they there from til?

The presents of a higher being demonstrates that man is intelligent enough to know he has an origin.

If guns were so bad, I do not think the National Rifle Association (NRA) would still be in existence.

If many people in an area die from starvation, do not let them regenerate.

Reproduction is perhaps the most important function of sex.

Every person has a different reason why he chooses his major, while some people have no reason at all.

Other symptoms are a paleness of the face and, if the victim is not treated promptly, death.

*Surely death is the **final** symptom.*

XV

Grim Grammar

. . . prose: words in their best order . . . .
~ Samuel Taylor Coleridge

My Room

As one enters my room, which is on the second floor of our house, may see a messed up place because my sister and I share the room. She is only nine and has things all over the floor as well as the furniture.

My bed is a double bed, in case of company my mother and dad sleep in it and I sleep on the davenport, and the furniture matching it. My sister has a single bed which I slept in when I was small. My bed is facing the door when my sister's is long ways between two windows.

Under my bed one may find shoes of all kinds because that is where I take them off and kick them under the closes thing I am near. One may find that dust has accumulated on them and when I want to wear a pair, I have to take time to clean them.

On the dresser, which is mine for use, I have a jewelry box and a little lamp with a red shade and globe. The vanity, which my sister uses for her playthings such as: dishes, paper and anything she may find, has a small white jewelry box, a small doll, and a picture of my dad when he was in the army.

The Chester drawer is standing behind the door one enters into the room and the closet. It is just small enough to fit into that small space. It contains the little things which can not be hung on a hanger. On its top one may find a small box, which I received from Penn Furniture Company for graduating from high school, and quite a few straight pins for hanging my shirts up with to put in the closet.

There is a small stand which stands under a window, which my sister uses as a desk when she is playing or writing papers to show her teacher.

The two mirrors, one on the vanity; the other, the dresser, are smeared with powder and cream because my sister puts it on herself as well as the mirrors, she looks in.

The closet is very small compared to all the clothes which have to be hung in its opening My dad, mother, sister and mine all have to go in the small space, as well as the boxes of my sister's toys and shoes of my mother and sister. The clothes become wrinkled and have to be ironed almost every time before we wear them.

Try to get your relatives out of the closet. There will then be more room for clothes.

The two windows are located in very good spots for the light off Oakland Avenue and from my uncle's house next door on the left. They are also in a good position to get the fresh air of the morning because the wind mostly blows toward the side or back of our house.

The room, itself, is about twelve feet by nine feet, which is almost as wide as the house is all but the bathroom. It is the largest room in our house.

The wall paper is of a dull flower design; the ceiling is of white wallpaper; and both of them haven't been changed since we moved into the house.

[The End]

He had on a new pair of hunting pants held up by suspenders and a faded blue shirt.

Do not carry gasoline in a can when going on vacation in the trunk of the car.

I most certainly shall not do so.

[student's evaluation of a fellow student's composition] Theme VI was a grammatically good written paper.

. . . a mink also snuck up behind him from the shore which sniffed him and slithered off.

I, when a youth, considered my parents' word law, and they expected me to obey when they gave an order, because it was for the betterment of me to obey. I, as usual, executed them with the utmost speed and perseverance.

The ship was immense and it lingered along in the water so slowly that I almost mistakably took it for a whale because it was dimly lit.

Henry Jame's wrote about people wearing social masks like those of England.

My dad's father was killed shortly after his birth.

The Korean conflict was still going on strong after graduating from high school.

In the afternoon I would take my homework swimming with me.

The high point of fan reaction to [outfielder Dave] Parker came during the 1980 season. While playing the first game of a doubleheader in Pittsburgh, a fan hurled a transistor battery at Parker that barely missed his head while playing right field. This outraged Parker as he took himself out of the game and the talk of a trade began.

Opening the freezer to get a gallon of vanilla ice cream, an arctic airblast hit my body and sent chills up my spine.

This plant is worth a million and one-half dollars.

Walking farther into the forest, birds are heard singing their bittersweet song of autumn.

Spitting green saliva and staring at me face to face, my heart stopped pounding and went blank.

Suddenly a rabbit comes hoping across the forest and hides under a bush from another.

My father's mother was living with us about three months when my mother learned that she was pregnant.

Taking care of grandmother who had to be spoonfed while she was pregnant was hard on mother.

Strolling along the lonely countryside, sheltered in warm clothing as the temperature fluctuates with the slightest of breezes, the rustling of leaves can be heard in the background.

Piled one on top of another in rows, I entered the trailer with my forks lowered.

After walking several hundred yards, music could be heard.

[from the Daily Bulletin] Lost—one black man's umbrella.

The Coast Guard recorded how the collision of these two ships occurred by radar.

Every day I hurried home to see his smiling face greet me running up the walk.

He had a crew cut which he wore on his head with flat sides.

Coming home from the city, the terrific blizzard roughed up the family.

Butch was sitting between Wimp and I holding the pizza we had just bought in his lap.

There is a person sitting at the table of the opposite sex.

After leaving the game he collapsed on the sidewalk and died without medical assistance.

Turning from the stove, Mom's smile warmed us all.

Students can profit from theme pre-correction in that the teacher can be on hand to discuss errors while in the process of being made.

A course was offered on the birth and care of mothers and babies.

As for the physical activities, I usually participate in as many as I can, for I am an out-of-doors lover.

Facing reality is a problem which many people do not do.

The bad rumors were about a few of the people that worked there but the majority were very nice.

His speech is slow and deliberate like he is trying to remember every detail. He mixes in his conversation small amounts of Pennsylvania Dutch, which give it a natural touch to the surrounding.

He had only one arm that hung loosely from his shoulder.

A week or two at most is spent on how babies are born in health class.

After lying in bed for two hours, the alarm clock rang.

Today, while driving through Florida, a bridge stands over 500 feet in the air.

Being right on the Vatican's doorstep, artificial contraception is declared illegal.

Proceeding from aisle to aisle, the brightly lit ceiling literally bounces off the freshly waxed floor into my eyes.

The impression he could throw you out the door without opening it stared you in the face.

Scopes was arrested for violating the state law which denied the right of a teacher to teach how man evolves in a public school.

Most of us do not realize what the rear of a building looks like when walking on the street in front.

The cows are milked and the meals prepared for the day on a charcoal or a wood fire.

Money is needed for life, but some can live with very little.

XVI

LONG LIVE MRS. MALAPROP

*The difference between the right word and
the almost right word is the difference
between lightning and the lightning bug.*
~ Mark Twain

Darwin's theory of evolution: the survival of the fetus.

I came to college in order to get a more contraceptive view of life.

The study of lung cancer and smoking is currently being carried on with pathological research.

He was jewish, and was not circumlocucious till he was twelve.

[of Pittsburgh-born poet
Robinson Jeffers] His underlying
view is that man and his works
are abdominable.   *Methinks this is a low blow.*

Some playwrights produce mellow dramas.

Probation was hard on Grandpa, because a bottle of beer was hard to find. But not to be denied, he set up a brewery in the basement. The house would ring with laughter and the odor of beer which oozed up through the floorboards and into all the rooms and finally right into the attic.

Seize Today: that is the Communist theory which will finally gain world denomination.

Don Juan was not trying to elude everyone into his corner.

Madame Bovary violated her marriage vowels.

King Lear's big problem was Regan and Gonnorhea.

[Shakespeare's Iago—again] He informs Brabantio of his daughter's elopement in a vile metaphor:
> Even now . . . an old black ram
> Is tupping your white ewe.

He further castrates the old man for his disbelief.

To have religion we must have faith in God and must believe in salvation and immorality.

The convict was dropped in his tracts.

In addition to this I became familiar with the habitat of certain small game and gained an understanding of when, where and with what trap to captivate them.

The Idiot [Dostoyevsky's hero] . . . disintegrated himself and fell back under the attack of epilepsy.

I now realize that love is a continuing process of discovering all the important faucets of an individual's personality.

This Was a Poet—an autobiography of Emily Dickinson. I forget who wrote it.

[Washington, D. C. in the spring] He expected to drive through the streets which would be polluted with cherry blossoms.

It's a doggie dog world.

[of Strindberg's Miss Julie] After breaking her engagement with a boyfriend, Julie's sex drive becomes uncontrollable and she begins inducing a valet.

Each granite of sand showed its thankfulness for the freedom from the heavy crowds of daytime.

Brigham, out of his love for the poet, excreted a monument in memory of Chaucer, in 1555.

[on poet William Blair's "The Grave"] I enjoyed excavating my ideas out of the poem.

I was not overly fond of horses and remembered that I still had to feed the blatant animals.

Syphilis pushed a rock up a hill that kept falling down and so he didn't have time to make love.

He was lucky he had time to think about it.

Scopes was teaching evolution in his high school biology class. They claimed that he was violating a state statue.

After regaining my composer I was able to complete my task.

Quite often, after their meetings, the fraternity guys would come to the union in a mass. They would conjugate in one corner and laugh and talk loudly, and sometimes get quite noisy.

Many black females, as well as males, are stagnant.

Svidrigailov's crime was that of the essentialist.

Self-hypnosis has many faucets, each of which can be limited into its infamous catesure.

[Novelist Thomas] Hardy interrupts life as he sees it.

[Novelist D. H.] Lawrence shows the wrongness of trying to dominate a person's life. We see that it can hurt the denominator as well as the denominated.

Insanity was quite popular in Shakespeare's time.

Sitting there in the synagogue I felt rather strange being the only genital present.

Philip [*Of Human Bondage*] treats Mildred for a venerable disease.

. . . high levels of nitrate in the water (which was proved to have come from nitrogen fertilizer) may increase the morality rate among female babies.   *Science will one day cast doubt on this.*

Certainly Ivolgin [in Mikhail Petrovich Artsybashev's *Nina*] is a fake and a freud.

They glanced at him in a way that anyone who is inquisitive would glance. But behind those glances was more than inquisition.

We see him on T.V. with his wife and lovely children. Everything is made to look so homely.

The Chinese are free-loving people.

After I had advanced half way through the play I became very indulged until I had finally finished.

Her skirt was like a protectorate for her legs.

Man wasn't able to live out of the water until ozone was formed to protect the earth from dangerous ultra-violent radiation.

Englishmen are not like men of other denominations.

Sam got much satisfaction out of his verbal dishortation.

When brought under control by humans, it [the environmental crisis] can be resolved, and man can live harmonically with the environment.

A certain girl dislikes her boss. Upon hearing his name she gets a discussed look on her face.

John Wayne, America's symbol of viral masculinity, is shown sporting a gold bracelet in the November issue of *Journal* magazine.

Sir John Suckling, who represents the cavalry poets . . . .

I suppose that I really shouldent have been concerned, but I am a repulsive worrier and this is my nature.

Etymology deals with the derision of words.

This piece of writing featured good illiteration.

An open mind is not a vacuum but a flexitivity.

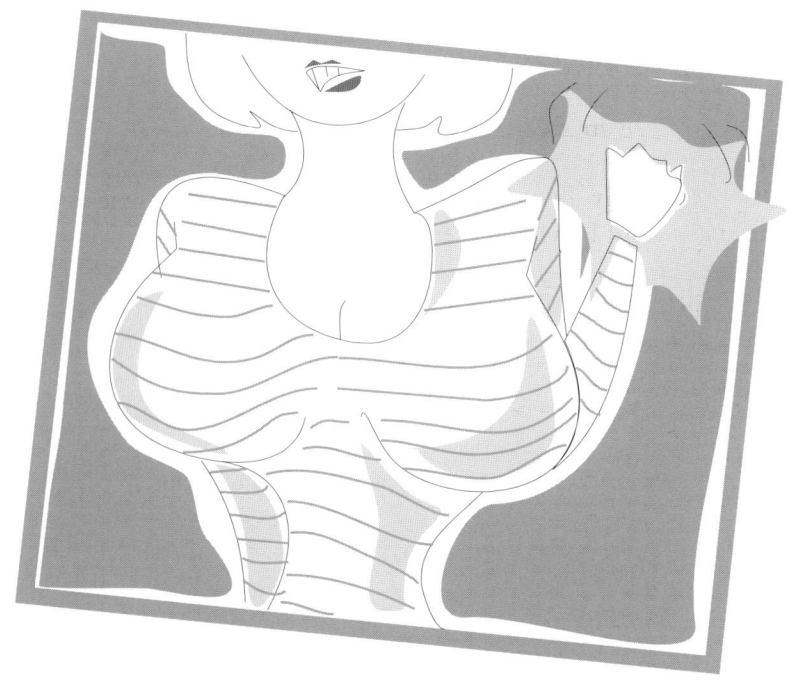

A woman's bust is the most prominent part of her body, a thing of beauty to be looked at flagrantly.

Robert Burns, quite a libertine himself, could appreciate the struggles of the French Revolution easily.

In my opinion an open mind is a prime subject for pollution.

But all of this is futile thinking. As a human being, I must face the trials and tribulations of life's cruel reality, and smile archaically.

[of Ishmael (*Moby Dick*)] His attitude toward death seems filled with faith in the immorality of the soul

Oedipus was a man guilty of the murder of his father and the adulteration of his mother.

[of Robert Penn Warren's short story "Blackberry Winter"] Jeb's mom had become fruitless.

Students nowadays are fighting for more precipitation in the administration of colleges and universities.

If a man is truly a gentleman he would not indulge in premarital relations because of the consideration he has for the party concerned. But this is not the case as indicated by the rousing increase in unwed mothers.

Were we ever lucky! It all turned out to be nothing more than an obstacle allusion.

XVII

THE WORD'S THE THING

How forcible are right words.
~ Job

In announcing that she would not be a candidate for re-election, Mrs. X said personal affairs will keep her too busy to run again. Up for grabs in the fall will be Mrs. X's seat.

Actually Monica was envious of the opposite sex because she thought the male demanded more respect than its human counterpart, the female.

As the ingot proceeds through the rollers, it becomes constantly thinner, until finally it is the proper thickness.

I became frightened and jumped behind a lilac bush to see what would happen.

I strode into the pool-room, determined to drown my troubles.

The most important aspect of a good leader is his execution.

When a girl wears a scanty costume she is really desirous.

Education at Brook Farm was quite advanced; the desire was for the students to enjoy frequent intercourse with the teachers.

The priest passed his water to the novitiate.

There is always a crowd at the beach full of different sights making you look frivorously around at all the wonderful scenery.

My grandmother suspended me on her lap.

Human nature is an uncontrollable trait.

There is a bit of sereneness in the air.

. . . accompanied by their two bewildered and expectant parents.

This child who is deprived of the proper guidance by his parents becomes sore at the world and the occupants within the world.

Country love and mother love are high on the list of ideals.

The Board of education held its monthly meeting yesterday at 7:00 p.m. The attendance was perfect.

[from the Daily Bulletin] Geography of U. S. and Pennsylvania Field Trip to Laurel Highlands: the time is Tuesday morning. Buses load at 7:30 to 7:35 and leave at 7:45 a.m. from the Circle. Dress is optional.

The highways leading out of London were littered with thieves.

It will take Raskolnikov [*Crime and Punishment*] a long time to become fully un-mixed up.

[advice to the student speaker] A good speech is improved through the addition of suggestive movement.

What is to become if there is no desire or ambition?

Their ages fluctuated between twenty and twenty-five years.

The student viewed his matter with a closed mind.

Raskolnikov's theory included the idea that the inferior segment of society was here merely to reproduce the earth.

Lois is always proud of her big seat.

Alice was getting married and the alter had been decorated suggestively.

. . . throughout my English career . . . .

She adored Frost and Shakespeare. Her scrapbooks were full of clippings and newspaper articles concerning English, poems and literature. This heap of junk . . . .

[discovered in a character sketch of a moody neighbor] One of the worst moods I ever experienced seeing him in was at the wedding of his daughter. At a time like that he should have felt very proud and happy. No, he couldn't be that way. He had to be very quiet and seductive. Maybe he didn't hurt himself as much as he hurt his daughter, but the least he could have done was to show some respect.

He knew the ecstasy of having lubricated a car for the first time.

His desires were slowly being shredded.

My boyfriend got so fresh I really let him have it.

Mrs. Warren, of Bernard Shaw's play, was a member of the oldest profession but was not a fallen woman but simply mislaid.

XVIII

ONCE a PUN a TIME

*A pun is a noble thing per se.
It fills the mind;
it is as perfect as a sonnet; better.*
~ Charles Lamb

*People that make puns are like wanton boys
that put coppers on the railroad tracks.*
~ Oliver Wendell Holmes

They had to work with their bare hands to make their ends meet.

I decided to take up agriculture because farming seemed to me to be a growing industry.

The odor of smoke could be smelt on my hands. *It could have been herring.*

Open-mindedness can be carried to far when it harms the welfare of other people. In New York City, a trial was held to determine if the topless waitress was decent. The verdict was in favor of the topless waitress. In this particular incident, open-mindedness came to the front by giving people the right to enjoy a good thing.

[deer hunting in the Pennsylvania mountains] Reluctantly he set his rifle against the tree and placed his hands in his coat pockets. He knew this was the wrong thing to do, but he couldn't withstand the cold any longer. Suddenly he froze.

Some men pray on women.

We carefully weighed out 900 grams and disposed of the balance.

[discussing his composition] I made an error in using "would," but he didn't degrade my paper.

Carol was one of the best-kept girls in town.

I felt that he was engaged in a very suitable occupation; he was a tailor.

Who is Yesua? ["A Walk in the City"] —a Jewish profit.

XIX

The Keen Observer

Innocent and infinite are the pleasures of observation.
~ Henry James

You can observe a lot by watching.
~ Yogi Berra

The cement sidewalks click with the sound of scurrying feet together with the frequent screeching of brakes of impatient drivers.

Sitting on the mud brown bench, a distint fire and coffee from the bagel wagon area fills your nose, as the short gusts of wind blows by.

The door handles were made of a dark brass finish.

Hearing the noise made by rabbits nearby, the deer looks around and scurries off through the trees.

Looking into my backyard, I could distinguish that fall had arrived for the leaves glimmered with brilliant colors of gold, orange and crimson and the few flecks of green in the golden sun.

A day in October is filled with solemn sounds, odors, sights and even people.

The few cars, travelling on the waterlogged roads, were visible only by sounds captured at the pause of thunder.

How many times have you observed a daisy going 55 miles per hour in a car?

Often enough, thank you.

Also these people can usually be recognized by the massive amounts of hair on their heads which includes beards and moustaches.

The silence became twice as silent.

Moving from left to right across the surface of the desk there is a Kleenex box with no Kleenex in it.

It was a cerebral hemorage wich started at the liver and worked its way to the head the cause steroids.

The tables and chairs are all approximately the same height and come to a halt before getting halfway to the top of the room.

Death occurs to everyone at some time during his life.

THE PROFESSOR HIMSELF, DISTRACTED AND RETIRED